The Unbeckonable Bird

¤

Pamela Murray Winters

FUTURECYCLE PRESS
www.futurecycle.org

Cover artwork, "The Taxi" by Olivia Moore; author photo by WillByington.com; cover and interior book design by Diane Kistner; Georgia text and Alegreya Sans titling

Library of Congress Control Number: 2018941385

Published by FutureCycle Press
Athens, Georgia, USA

ISBN 978-1-942371-97-7

Now you can make believe on your tin whistle,
You can be my broom-boy.
Scrub me till I shine in the dark.
I'll be your light till Doomsday.
Black cat cross your path,
Why don't you follow.
My claw's in you and my lights in you
This is your first day of sorrow.

Richard Thompson, "Calvary Cross"

For Rob

Contents

Your Healing Finds You

*"If you pour some music on whatever's wrong,
it will sure help out."*
—Levon Helm

Better yet, approach it:
    boldly, like a gymnast to the bars. Or gently:
        surgeon to suture, child to chile pepper,
    fingers to first skin.

Whatever way, you can't grasp it
    as yours. It's not a salve, so it can't
        go back in the bottle.
    You can dance with it for a little while.

You can soak in it, let it change your color,
    make you giddy, make you ache.
        You go into it, or it chooses you.
    The topical is not enough.

You can look for it, but more likely
    it'll light on your head,
        fly too soon. Or, if you're blessed,
    it'll rise in you, well in you:

innumerable animalcules
    unbeckonable, bound
        to kill death,
    to make you whole.

The Sylvia Plath Tattoo

is a curious cat, or somebody's idea
of a bell jar. Occasionally

it's flowers. Sometimes it eats men
like air. It's umbrella, it's kettle,

it breaks from the box or the mind.
It's a portrait too pale, insipid blonde

in an Alice band, made grave
by the frame some other inker chose.

It's a bone fragment, a smear of blood
or ink. An elbow, an eye. Half

a line, four pearls, a handful of dactyls,
a wisdom tooth. A dried-out,

blued-out petal remembering the tulip.
Always, it says, like any scar: *I am.*

Mine

Takoma Park, Maryland, 1970

Out past the greasers' corner and the four-way stops
is the end of the nine-year-old earth:
the Savage Market. Savage long gone, it's run by Joe:
fat man, invisible cigar, heap of a belly,

the boss who palms our mothers' pay
and returns our five-cent pickles
from the dim swimming jar,
our candy rocks and jawbreakers, our foamy tonics.

We always come in from the back, up the alley
by the Gilhooly house (the one that burned,
Mom said, for insurance), around the front
where Joe sits, back to the window,
finger-quick eyes on the stock.

Sometimes, I let the kids with more coin
go on ahead. I stop by the shade of the green iron bin
and gather the spills:

half-shiny caps, crown-edged, each with its bright legend.
Nehi, Dad's, Crass, Crush. Sometimes
a strange make calls: some root beer, usually,
from a place I'll never travel,
or its exotic kin, sarsaparilla.

I hold them in my hands, study. I press
their teeth into my white girl-palms. I turn them over.
Sometimes I pick at the cork insides,
looking for their secrets:
numbers, cork-bit runes, a dull half-mirror.

Omphaloskepsis

It's the hole that's not a hole, the cave
of the smallest childhood mysteries
and milky lint like the nest of a worm
who graduated to moth and fled
to eat the world. Can we not evolve
past it and its ex-purpose?

It's been cut, pierced, banned, stuffed,
draped, flaunted. Seeing it, unexpected,
on a friend, leads to liquored thoughts,
flighty desires. Could we enter it
and be new again, ignore the reality
of its unseen terminus?

And how is it a button? Vestibule, chakra,
chocolate cherry, apple cleft, shot glass,
goat's eye. End of a balloon. Yes.
We are our mothers' balloons, cut off
and flown like drunkard moths
to hungry openings.

The Problem With Chickpeas

The problem with chickpeas isn't
their mutability, their waxy-hard faces
turning soft in the rising embrace
of bubbles. They lay down their lives
to save a sentient protein, disembody
in the hymn of hummus. They have

many names: garbanzo, cicer, Indian pea,
chana, sanaga pappu. They were prayer beads
for Rumi, and their name, to him,
is hidden from us. Small imperfect
spheres, collapsing planets, transformative
clay: their problem is not the ways

they change. It is that they are
humble flesh, cheap in the can, and we cooks
expect so much from them.

Cardiac

As I lie on the table, I think about flying
on that chill airline with the colored lights. Like
Alien: suspended in time and air. I try
to believe I'm flying, somewhere beautiful.

The instrument probes; I feel the technician's
sweater against my bare waist, the warmest
black can be. She tells me before
she touches my breast.

There are vignettes of sound,
like wipers in heavy rain. From what
I can tell, an even rhythm. Then
one set, at the hard center,

urgent, knocking. All the while I sense
her corona of dark hair, her sweater,
her care. I wonder what her touch
tells her about my heart, or whether

all insight is in the wires, the probe. I
seem to be normal, she tells me,
as she wipes the gel, removes
the leads. She doesn't know me. As I

drive home, a light rain is falling, and
I remember the astronaut Ripley
and her companion, the cat: travelers
we see who can't see, alive and sleeping.

Hoisting the Pretend Sail

Later I learned my favorite home was *away*.
My favorite songs came in tabletop jukeboxes

in bus stations en route to the tombs of unknown cousins.
My favorite candies were the ones you broke with a hammer

or both your hands. Bark, brittle, sugar rock, the necklace
that rained the rainbow o's with the snap of a cord.

They'd dent your palms, draw blood in the mouth, and,
later, raise welts on the tender buds. Drunk on Dad's Root Beer

and being five and a half, I'd collage a life
from the rings and swords that fell from the gumball slot.

Not for me the chewy cherry cigar, the white-powder
smokes. I wanted handfuls, foreign cargo, salvaged

moments on my tongue. And not for me the life you earn
but the one you collect: bits, bins, barnacles. But that

was away, when my mind was loose as the sea, as young
as the sea was old, when I could say *I'm a princess,*

a pirate, a tabby cat and make it so. Adulthood:
this is the worst trip.

Landlords

My home was a piece of an old Victorian.
We were Apartment One. There were
four others: sometimes young families,

night nurses, girls who embroidered their jeans,
a carpenter who made wicked toddies for Mom,
a "brother and sister" who weren't,

an old woman who died there, a young man
in Apartment Four and then his neighbor.
It was the Seventies when Apartment Three

bought the house from the family across the street,
Mom's old Baptist friends, and had the walls
torn down between. We knew

he and Apartment Four had been friends,
hadn't guessed they wanted to share a home.
They gave us a tour. Later there were sneers

and who's-the-wifes. There was almost a fruit plate
for Christmas before someone thought better.
Did I laugh? Did I defend? I was busy

with being plain and being unable to catch
a man of my own. I loved the landlords,
their mustaches, their shiny showy cars.

Was it the luck of where I slept that they
enchanted me? Forty years on, what stays: nights
in my bed against the wall, back when I thought

I had to pray for everyone lest they or I be lost,
and when I begged for a boyfriend and a pert nose,
and my dreams went up past the attic, and

down came the music of the grand
piano and of men, every night, singing
as if their lives depended on it.

For Robin Williams

When he lived, the bird could come
  at whim or goodwill. He'd purr and warble
like a catbird, soar around the back door
  and over the poles, down

  to Mesopotamian coprolites—
the old shit—and into each of the rooms
  of the heart. We thought that medicine
could help. The scalpel slips. *The patient*

failed, the medical journals say, not to blame
  God or the AMA. Some things are bigger
than celebrity. I've heard the golden Oscar
  is lighter than a human brain. After Walt

  Whitman died, the surgeons wanted
to find his genius, but one of them, lifting
  the massive organ, dropped it. Like Robin's, it
contained multitudes. Surely

from jump, from spring, our redfuzz bird
  babbled and burred, Celtic
in tone as a stone you have to hang
  upside down to kiss,

  American in wingspan as the big sky
with clouds in it. *There's one*
  that looks like a horse, you'd ponder,
and this bird, loosed,

would dart up and a stallion
  would leap before you. You'd forget,
as it flew, that only in a race
  are all hurdles

the same. And now
we want to grab the mane and
     keep moving. Maybe handstands
in the saddle, not to show off,

just to feel the lift of the gallop.

No Mud, No Flowers

There's a reason it cakes on your shoes:
misery loves company. One clod

can't just skip over the creek or attract flies
by itself: it wants to spread, the world

its bagel. It wants you to taste it and know
where it came from. For all it knows,

it might taste like chocolate, and if you
don't know, you might find it sweet.

Just know it bears you no malice. It's just
in desperate need of its own fame.

It'll never be the fringe tree, the mimosa,
the white rose. Poor sad lonely hate.

For Jesse, Visiting "Small Stories" at the Building Museum

I'm trying to remember your face on the other side
of the dollhouse. I was outside, looking in. You,

on the open side, had no wall; you were with
the small chairs, the tiny piano,

looking for the chicken, looking for
the footman, pressing the button

to keep the lights on. *One of the things
I love,* you'd said earlier, *is the inconsistency*

of scale—this as we regarded the coronation
of Elizabeth II, rendered in paper cutouts:

the wavy red carriage and its fine
huge horses, the grooms barely reaching

the horses' knees. Then: the Paper Shtetl.
The Rabbi encircled his text, head and arms cut

from a single circle folded just so, so much
within that embrace. A wobbly cart, too poor

for a donkey—too poor, even, for woodgrain
on both sides of the sheet. The flat dancers

curved through the scene. Black and white lines,
no color. (Friends for twenty-odd, and

I don't know the color of your eyes. I never
met them through the dollhouse window.)

This is my favorite, I said. *So much joy from
mere paper.* You replied, *Well, we are*

the People of the Book.

Parrot

Settling into the dark, she rehearses: *Hello. Do whatcha wanna. Hello?*
  I'm sorry.
Brrrr. You don't know Jack! I love you. Does it please her,

this pearl necklace of phonemes? My mother never made me kneel for
  prayers;
I lay in bed and singsonged *Now I lay me* and the rest, a canticle in which

the first sounds I knew as words were *sleep* and the names of all I wanted
  God to bless,
not forgetting Cleo the stuffed rabbit. I wonder how old I was

when I balked at saying the third line because I recognized *die*. What was
  this thing
that might kill me in the night, might waver over taking my soul? Later,

I took to saying it all except *die,* that syllable of surprise you can't say
  quietly.
I left a space, a rest. I don't know if parrots revise their repertoire.

Ours doesn't talk, but she whispers at bedtime. I haven't heard her, but
  my love
tells me it's so. My love tells me, and it's a good story, and so I believe.

Meat Cove

We went because the name made us snicker,
four Americans in someone's dad's motor home,

careening around the Cape roads, singing
folk tunes. One of us was learning bagpipes. The whine

of his practice chanter paused for lunch. The picnic table,
on a plateau halfway down to the Gulf of St. Lawrence,

was dramatic but too much for us; we ate
our groceries at the dinette. Headed out, someone

spotted two kits, too bright to be camouflaged. We stopped.
They came to us, a few feet from the high window.

Their small colorless eyes beseeched. Missing
our pets at home, we agreed—despite the warning signs—

to offer up the rest of the rotisserie chicken
bought in Antigonish. As it fell into the brush, three more

young foxes appeared. Now I understand the words *snarl*
and *worrying,* as in shaking a living thing, predator's jaws

closed on prey's convenient part, until the life snaps.
The cooked meat flew, the small bones. We left before

we saw blood.

Shake, Alabama

I want to be Brittany's dress. I want her
to hold me to her breast as she shakes
and makes my fringes dance. If I could

dissolve on her like lacquer, run
through her like liquor, OK, but I'd
rather be her frock, a flour sack

or rayon shift with flowers. A kick
in the gut, wraiths tangling with
a wolf—you'd think these would be

the consequence of that voice, that mouth,
that whole body of song, but her shimmy
remakes it into joy. I don't just want

to be filled with that flame; I want to
flaunt, to strut, to burn. I want the scale
to zip up my back and zing.

Mallows

I grew up, in the middle states, with a hollyhock,
or so I thought. It was lavender-pinkish,

with papery leaves. Its blooms grew
deeper at their centers. Showoffs, I thought, flowers

of more than one color. Now I see postvirginal's
a better word, as the pollen speckles the heart.

                I know now
that what my mother called periwinkles
were a kind of violet, her bluebells and pinkleberries

small weeds. When I first saw a hibiscus, I doubted
my mother's nomenclature, who called herself

hillbilly, wallflower, homely—a word
that in England is an embrace.

                My mother chose
Pamela, "a name for a rich, spoiled English girl."
How could she know I'd love a country she never saw?

But she could tell a hibiscus from a hollyhock,
one exotic, one clutching the porchpost, both mallows,
dark at the heart.

Adulterous Conceit at 3 a.m.

I would wrap myself in damp weeds, kelp, my best green dress.
I would feed you four mimosa seeds and keep the pod.

We would tangle across the lawn, bushes and briars,
consuming the siding, cracking the chimney.

Or you would need it so much you couldn't speak.
I would be too perfect. Church bells and you'd wither.

Or the tears would make the bed a boat, carry us into town,
and we would be judged and fined and fettered.

Or you would grow young and be my child,
head in my apron, your knees crooked and cold.

Or I would say no yes no but no, and
shave my head, and bend to you, and hate us both.

Or we could never talk about movies again.
Or you'd forget my name and we could start over.

Excuse me, sir. Pardon me, ma'am. Enveloped,
pillars of fog, mine an illicit smoke. Or the Bible

would flop open and Sarah, wife of Abraham,
would laugh. They say I glow. Sunlight I dreamed.

On Seeing the Word "Ether"
in Lorna Luft's Memoir

I wasn't scared. I was warned about the mask
and that I would go to sleep. What I can't remember
is the smell. Maybe like shiny gowns,

the sort of freezers defrosted with picks and cake pans,
empty tubes of lipstick. They don't use it now—
too volatile. In her memoir, Lorna Luft said her mother

was never a drunk; it was all pills, and people
used to think they were safe. The spin doctors,
the drugs we don't talk about, the "exhaustion," the

"out of control," the cuts and tucks, the innumerable
tiny explosions on elevators: too often we lie
about what makes a star. Or we do what seems best

at the time, what the experts choose. In London, Judy
called the queen's doctor for her daughter's sickness,
who said there was nothing wrong. It was

Lenny Bruce's doctor who found the girl's appendix
about to burst, saving Lorna's life. A commoner,
I was unscathed by my ether, too young to know

the crapshoot of history:
maybe we lose our tonsils,
maybe the hospital burns.

The Essential Man

Leonard Cohen, Columbia, Maryland, May 13, 2009

Sent ahead in some rental truck:
purple and silver-gold drapes like streamers
for a prom in Baltimore
or hell

and a Persian rug to pray on
and battlements and wires we needn't see
because everybody knows
it's the man
who makes things move.

He generates the Elvis leg. He does the
Toronto tarantella. He flaunts the
pizzicato beret. He flanks the
Sho-Bud pedal steel. He cradles

kindness and the microphone
in palms gentle as an old lover's breath.
He instigates two blonde cartwheels,
quick and gone. He testifies to
the rose that lies
fourteen inches ahead of his toe.

His knee balances the sky.
He is an orchestra of left hands
pressing keys, clasping chords,
beckoning to follow,
collecting what falls
for an instant, then letting
it fall. He is down

to essence: the servants beside
and before, the nails on his
fingers and toes, the song

that swells him
to sail us over the festoons,
through the Northern Territories,
straight off the map.

It Seemed a Good Idea

for Richard Thompson

Your face on an old magazine, Bee's scanner,
a maneuver easy to pull off.
We, the audience, put your face over our own
so when you came onstage at the Birchmere there were
a hundred of yourself staring back.
Now I see it: who wouldn't have been perturbed?

            We'd worked on your faces
all the previous afternoon, affixing each cutout
to a paint stirrer. Then Bee, using a Phillips head,
had carefully made eyeholes. It seemed a good idea
at the time, to be able to see.

            (The faces have lingered.
People have brought them to later concerts,
in other cities. One face took up residence
in the sound booth, where a year later—
I swear we wanted the best for you,
and ourselves—the front man of some prettyboy
cigarette band brandished it onstage, to laughter.)

            We thought you'd laugh.
Your bassist did, and the sound man, and
several ushers. We intended love, to immerse you
in our joy at you. I should have known better,
but Bee was innocent, a lark, in the post-show
schmooze line, who shook your hand
and said *Hi, I'm Bee, and I spent last night
poking out your eyes with a screwdriver.*

Accidental

during Richard Thompson's "Uninhabited Man"

As you listen to the song
　　and watch its rainwashed
　　　　coast spill away from you
　　　　　　like a runner carpet,

two of your fingers
　　touch your lips,
　　　　your hand perpendicular
　　　　　　to the lip line,

and it's a kiss.
　　Skin meets, softly,
　　　　crosswise. You wonder
　　　　　　if smokers

do it for this delicate buss,
　　a shy press of flesh, potential
　　　　openings. A sly sign
　　　　　　for hush. There's

that song again—
　　it hasn't stopped.
　　　　It's part of this moment
　　　　　　between yourself and accident.

You want to
　　move to a country where everyone's
　　　　first kiss is this one, surrounded by rain,
　　　　　　almost safe, still breathless.

Small Repair

The man in tweed on the TV
on the dentist's ceiling
says we once had two souls,
a big one and a little. I think it's the little
one that hides or flees
when I'm getting my teeth fixed, in tests
requiring stirrups, and when I sleep.

        To sleep is to trust
the waking. You could always
go down one staircase too many
and not come up. Sleeps are my remedy
when I crave stopping,
my small pseudosuicides. Healthy
for now, despite the dental evidence,

        I know my little soul,
which flashes and tumbles and
loves, could use a trim. Shaggy,
reminiscent of the mission kitchen
and the posters of the lost,
it needs to straighten up, grow up,
be here, and stop hurting.

        Only the last is the one
I resist, the one that would make
little soul into big, the unpersoning of
the unknown. Finished, tooth number 8
looks like its neighbor at 9, as if I never
thrashed in some dream and spoke
the unspoken, chipping it away.

Dave and the Wolverine

for Dave Carter (1952-2002)

Tall, Tantric-tantrum-haired, receding backward, or maybe "backward"
was a memory I made up after I knew it was the last time I'd see him.
He probably just walked away, toward the offstage door, and I smack
my fool head, figuratively, at that too-easy metaphor. I saw his last show
two days before his heart stopped. I hate the pride I felt at that fact. Give
me a badge; I've paid my rock-and-roll dues. I met him four or five times;
a real journalist would remember. I teased him about karaoke, sought his
insights on cannabis. I saw Joan Baez, who will herself never die, dance
with him. He called her a dakini. I had to look it up: "a Tibetan timeless
inorganic immortal non-human being." Did Joan, who has danced with
sixty years of songcatchers, see it coming? I never saw it coming. Did he,
that lanky folky prophet with the exalted eyebrows, the square-dance
shirts, the transcendental banjo strap? Did he, polymorphous polyglot
head-case balladeer, full of secrets shot through with a little sweet snake
oil, see it coming? Risen in the morning, out for a run, dead before noon.
Here's what Tracy wrote: *He came back for a lucid minute or two to
tell me, "I just died...Baby, I just died...." That's the true story I am going
to tell.* Truth is gnarly, like the tanglewood tree in his song. Four days
later, I had—or made up; hard for artists to tell—a dream: he was legging
it up a path that veered to the left, around a mountain. From off to the
right came a wolverine; it sank its claws into his shoulders, and he piggy-
backed it around the corner and out of sight. I don't know from wolver-
ines. I know what I thought a wolverine was, when I dreamed or imagined
it: small and sharp, feral-scented fur, a vicious tenacity. Could be he was
chased by the word. *Wolverine:* his earthly love, his o-my-darlin'; or his
story, trailing his shade, each bronze hair a tiny flame.

Sweet Cider Beloved

You will never know
that all the roads
line after line
led across your hand

and when you took the apple
red against white
skin against skin
your palm printed the world

so when you pressed it
to your mouth
you swallowed
your fortune

fresh cider and time
dripping from your fingers
gold in your throat
and the road
and home

Presbyterian Takoma Reverie

Balustrade. A tear. A trade. A grommet. Pick up the gimp and pull it
through. Hand off. Jerk off. Circles. Quick shears snip. Cut the ribbon

and christen the ship. Knuckles on the balcony rail. People faint
in church all the time. Daddy'd sleep; I'd save him with an elbow.

Alleluia less human than hallelujah. Sharp exhale. Relief. Tea leaves.
Trading a fortune for a four-wheeler. Dangerous when high. My town

was righteous and squirming, tumescent with the time. Circles
are socialist. Circles are families. Circles bounce when dropped,

provided they land on the edge. Daddy driving fast, car skips the sudden
hill, my stomach drops, better than sex would be. What did Romeo

look like, down on the terrazzo in his blue velvet swag, some squat fool
in the sunset of the west fumbling for his homily,

as Juliet, bathed in her own bright spot, embodied beauty? Her cells
spun. Could she even see him, below and at worship?

A Certain Field

I want to go back to a certain field, where there are stones
    but no trees.
I want to drop to my knees

    and rake and dig. I want to go deep
and pile high and maybe
    bleed. When I have twenty years,

I'll take them back.
    I'll throw myself into them
and do what I didn't. I'll sing. I'll fuck. I'll

    surrender and double back
and vanquish. Did I mention
    that I'll be beautiful? Soon the time

will be gone again, and my hands healed
    and clean, but I'll know
where they've been; I'll know

what they've done. I'll
    braid my fingers, step into them,
rise up.

Exegesis of a Bootleg Tape of "Truckin'"

It's not something you wear out:
not the interview suit, not the dress
to catch a swain. No, it's your favorite
PJs, with the hole where you scratched your ass
one too many times, the cotton-whitened coffee stain
you can still taste if you suck at your own breast pocket,

that ghost of the button that jumped ship
in the washer, and the tipsy string
where the tag once hung. You no longer remember
size or maker, composition or directions;
all that this rag-end gives you
is the small red splotch on your nape
where it rubs as you toss.

"What if everyone who ever abandoned us was carried off by fairies?"

In some darkness, over a border and on
damp ground, within a ring of blue-eyed Marys,

they shuffle and smoke: the men who went
for cigarettes in the Seventies, still thirty-four

and coughing. There is music, but it's not
their favorite—where's the bass, the

speed licks, the sax?—and they can't
change the station. If they still had speech,

they'd say they don't know how to dance.
Then a few will realize it's okay for a man

to put his hands on another man's shoulders
or waist, okay to betray a knowledge of rhythm.

Some of these men will dance right out of the circle
into a new world. Others will pause,

light another Kool. None of them will fight.
It's not much like the world we've made.

Watching Game Shows, Early Morning, Living Room

Gray faces, gray eyes, gray couture beaming down
from some satellite as if from a planet
where it's always 1953.
Gray, but not dead:

Arlene's earrings bounce, Steve's wit zings,
Joan's arm thrusts the pick-me wave
of every teacher's pet.
Horn-rim glasses.

Cigarette ads. Spray deodorant in swank bottles.
Swanson dinners. A parade of gray ordinary
people, innocent of Living Color,
let alone YouTube.

It's those humans—women in stick-pinned hats, pimpled
smart alecks, squirming immigrants
condescended to, coddled, handled
like unexploded bombs

by the horn-rim men in Cardin and Vitalis—
who seem most like aliens, recovered
from some lost world where no one knows
when to look at the lens,

when to look away.

How to Speak to the Dead

Don't hurry. Compose your thoughts. Assume
they know more than you do, but avoid
pointless questions. Use your own language,
even if it's not theirs. You don't have to whisper
but, if it feels right, do.

Don't wait for an answer. Like the living,
they may be diffident, mysterious, or rude.
Or there may be other sounds in the way.
Listen for sounds of all kinds, as well as
for things that are not sounds.

You should not have to pay for this encounter.
Nor will you receive an invitation.
If you love your voice, love your voice.
They, too, would love it, if they could.

Oliver Schroer's Last Invention

He gave it all away—the clothes, the books,
the thousands of tunes he plucked from the air
or got from the old fiddlers. What light he had
he pressed into the palms of schoolchildren.

I have his image, black on yellow, over my desk,
a stencil of his mohawked head years before
the cancer: "Canada's tallest freestanding fiddler."
He left a video, not with music, in which he removes

his beard, not with a razor but with his fingers.
Cycling through the styles, he gives them names:
*the weird artiste, hair-basket, muttonchops, bulldog
after a fight, Scruffums the Beard-Boy.* His last

invention, last instructional recording. *Finger shaving.
It's easy, it's painless, you don't cut yourself.*

Hunch

I grew up in a faith without saints,
so it shouldn't surprise that I don't know
what to feed them

or what they are supposed to do.
I've learned how to find them: by their
dull-smooth goodness, or their trees

strung up with little epiphanies,
or the smell of orange. They are not
ghosts, but they hover. They

seem to wait. Sometimes a muse,
when dead, transmogrifies: there is a red bell
in the heart that rings other such bells

and certain votaries tremble. Thus
are tribes made, congregations of
human islands gone evergreen—

I've made it up. I no more understand
this bond than I understood, at five,
how a car moves. Daddy would hunch

over the steering wheel; I supposed it was
his posture that instigated the motion
or maybe his will to travel.

Whip-Smart

You are silver fair, Liz Phair, you are toffee
as the notes fall, but hard-cockish at the middle
where you wield the wood. Did no one tell you
nice girls don't play guitar? It's boys
who work with gauges and circuits,
single-coil mysteries, humbuckers,
wang bars. Those belled flares, the shiny
white leather, thoroughbred hair, that
hell-black kohl—they're all for the Thors
and Apollos, the rock men, to brandish. And you,
you make us think twice: maybe they're not
built for it, maybe those Zeppelins and Stones
get in the way. Phair Liz, bare and sleek
and supernova, shake down the rain
from your wildcat eyes, fill the flask
with flange as you, whip-smart, shift your hips,
the room, that frat boy at the bar.

A Rose

I am learning to feel ever so slightly sorry
for the terribly beautiful:

that they are seldom alone
and never invisible;

that they will not have had to learn young
to be smart or pious;

that they will be helpless or desperate
against the years' erosion.

You think I'm elaborately mean,
but I try. I see them minimized,

lissome executive summaries of humanity,
personalities subsidiary to that glow.

Do the old ones carry small photos
of their earlier selves, flash them,

discreetly, at cashiers and postmen?
Still, give my history a year

of perfect nineteen, helpless to chase the gazes,
skin mildly sore from the becoming blush

prompted by whispers. How would it
change me at fifty to have known

the limber, lithe, unblemished pain?

In Which I Am Mad at Flowers
Because Paul Is Dying

The iris was drooping by the steps when I found it,
ripped, roots and all, from a neighbor's yard.

I carried it to work, filled an old bottle from the tap,
stuck it in. Its inner petals—they're called *standards,*

a friend told me—lay in a heap. Arranging them
with index nudges, I wondered whether I did damage,

as with a butterfly or fledgling. But you can't damage
what's already dead, I guess. Forty minutes later,

it rises from the green bottleglass, standards perked,
the lower petals—called the *fall*—splayed like hands

of some cartoon alien, purple with impossibly
delicate lifelines on sun-yellow palms. Looking at it,

limber, succulent, self-possessed as a zombie,
rattles the shards under my ribs, where easy love once was.

Bootleg Dharma

They came from JetPaks, from boxes, from the pockets
in the trousers of Paul, who last danced in oh-nine.

Made before I knew him, or the music, or much else,
this one tape sounds as if Paul, younger than I ever

knew him, lowered Edison, tinfoil cylinders, the lot
in a rotting bucket on a fraying rope down a mucky well

under Bristol's Three Jacks Club, torn down in '87.
My friend's very English murmur can be heard behind

the shush of his big warm hand concealing the mike. Where
did he hide it? The machines used to be so cumbersome.

On these plastic-cased coils of evidence—I have hundreds—
of decades spent illicitly trapping as much memory

as can be done on earth, Our Hero sings the old songs, and
the songs new then: "Vincent Black Lightning," "Bad Monkey,"

"Sweetheart on the Barricade." Here's Philadelphia, '94,
where Paul and I sing together, and late-summer wind

blows and whistles. Collection's a strange pursuit. Sometimes
the voices you know crowd you, twisted, as if you're earmuffed

or too far gone to care. Others are almost live. *I guess it's
possibly a bit unusual,* Paul said, on his last recording,

the one he made in the hospice, *for someone who's dead
to speak with you.* That one's perfect fidelity, but I prefer

the old ones, the analogs, bootlegged from devices
in tampon boxes and Tilley hats, the stuff of life bumping up

against them, their remove reminding us, the beachcombers
who pulled the cork from the bottle, that this was a single singing,

though not a single song.

I dreamed of taffeta—

or was it tulle? From the names,
tulle is smoother. This one danced
on the feet, on the tongue.
Burned a little. I dreamed

of gabardine, in web-decked bottles
in the cellar, smelling of prunes.
Seersucker, smartass, off for a hang
with Gatsbys. Broadcloth,

oatmeal, homework. Velour,
a chair into which you sink
and never rise again. Corduroy:
I'll save you!—he slays the foe

but you run off with cashmere.

The Moth on the Movie Screen

The guitarist Davey Graham has a mole on his cheek. His notes
so heartfelt, he seems present, even in black and white.
It's this shimmer in his face—which turns out to have flown in:
small wings, small body, darker than the preserved past.

We're in a barn on a resort. Has there ever been
hay here? Guitarists, Englishmen, singers, and acolytes
watch the old films under the pale light
of paper lanterns. Twice, people who are in the room

show up on screen, their younger selves. So many others
are dead: the bluesman with my father's drawn face
and the knuckles bigger than anything in the room.
The impresario. The journo. The comedian. The fiddler.

And now and again I see that small visitor,
craving the glow in the face of Marion Montgomery
or the glint in Martin Carthy's ear. Or who knows what?
It roams the Midland hillside, Seeger's studio.

There over the hours of the present, the decades
of the past. In a song, the move from one stanza
to the next can be real time or a century
in the singer's hands. And as my gaze wanders,

as I grow old, as Carthy the corporeal dozes, wakes,
stretches, rises, leaves the barn, as Peter Cook
and Dudley Moore spar for so long everyone's
got a beard, I realize that the wanderer might be

not one moth but a series of moths, their descending
and departing gone unnoticed.

I Am Background

Once I landed next to a dreadlocked,
jerseyed man who didn't talk
or even look: hands in the air, moving

as if hearing voices. But this was our job:
seeing things we were told were there.
This was our job yesterday,

in a stadium, cheering for a game
that happened in each of our heads. Above,
at a blank screen, we'd look for the kiss,

and we'd sigh for the clinch
we imagined. A stagger of emotion, ragged
cheers. They can fix it all in post.

Fewer than a hundred extras
to fill the bleachers, we became
a sort of human snake, coiling

and uncoiling our way, at the director's vision,
through every section of stands. We'd change
hats, props, hair. And once I ended up

with a high school friend,
a man I hadn't seen in thirty-some years:
for a shot or two, *background* to *cut*,

a companion. We had real history
but no time: next, the black-bobbed
woman again, the one who'd

done background for years. Jaded,
a little above the rest, she'd nevertheless
poke me at *Action!* as if I'd lived

next door, and grin,
mouthing words that weren't words.
Some men, the older ones,

took temporary wives, laughing
about it between takes. A bunch, a scatter,
and then another bunch. Is this

acting? I've seen dark birds
move against an afternoon
spelling in the sky: they go somewhere,

choose formations for ease
of travel, not for show. I guess if time
ran fast enough, they'd fill the sky black.

Maryland Yellow

late November 2018

Surely the Garden of Lovingweirdness
lies along a four-lane road in Maryland,
not so much a Scenic Highway Trail

as a trip south to north in a state that's both,
down whose shoulders squat the hotel,
St. Something's church, the eating place.

Every now and then that flag: Renaissance
meets racetrack. Red and yellow, black
and white. Two weeks ago the citizens

entered the school to cast their ballots.
No fights broke out. Poll workers
laid odds on the turnout; to the winner

went Old Bay peanuts, a donation
from one of the election chiefs.
Didn't matter which party. As they cross

the lot this afternoon, lips tight as a
live oyster, folks twist in their navy
windbreakers, buffalo plaids, bent denim,

shit-edged boots. They might have worked
nowhere, voted for no one. They want only
to fetch the mail, to bring the dogs home.

Imagine that flag, not heraldry but
patchwork, to be torn. Division stitched bright,
then ripped. This lonesome day

a woman drives: her car, her state, a shell. She's
of and not of it. Things happen. So tired,
she could let go; so much she can't carry,

can't unravel. She might let the road bend,
the whole balled-up lot of it lead her
right into the trunk of that oak tree,

but there's a snippet of yellow cloth
borne up. Look. There's a bird.

Conjuring Mark Sandman

of the band Morphine, who died onstage
playing two-string bass

Mark your low rock your croon rock me Sandman
down by the dock where you sank the ferry
down in the dell where the red bell rings belly to belly
round the corner and crack the sidewalk lead foot flyer.

Your hands are green and dusty rocking me Sandman
your hands are green and black and down my back and down
you go down where the secrets leach through rock and break
the earth and moan them into mist to suck and stone us.

The butt, the heel, the box, the trunk, the root.
The flower, the song, the gift, the god, the light.
The ventricle, the miracle, the pentothal, the Pentecost,
the cost, the debt you pay, the rent party, the death-pledge—

your rock is a house, your voice is a window, you chill me
with sacral somnambulant Sandman dreams
wet as life, hard as bone, tinnitus tenacious as an itch,
a blush, hot skin, dead Mark, low rock me.

Big Snooker

inspired by Pete Townshend's "Rough Boys" video

In the years before the plague, you, like many, saved on buttons,
shoved your chest against the wood and felt the power

uncoil through you. So lit on it, you'd smash and shatter
just to see the shards shine as they fell.

You said you hoped to die but didn't. You saw the others
flying like TVs from penthouse rooms, falling like skeet.

Folded sticks, slick cues, the clatter across the green felt
like horses. A point of impact that vanishes in the explosion.

Kind eyes and careless errors, searching the gutters
for stubs of what you were, for validation.

Was it God's thumbs that pulled down the corners
of your eyes, his needle that shot the sob into the wail?

Love was that last buddy at the bar.
The empty glass is testament to how he filled you.

Born in Deep Ellum

Luther's singing about keeping your lamp trimmed and burning
but Cody's turned his back to us on his drum throne
and combs his thin hair with his black comb
into a wet DA. Cowboy hat aside, with a towel
he wipes and grooms, elbows like a cat.
Like he's forgotten the show—or he's ready
for the spot. 'Cause Luther's got the music
running up and down those long legs,
fingers, face, but Cody is the music.
Some accident in utero, some slip,
and he's unhinged—all out, no in—

and Luther will learn everything, will lean
and yearn and swoon, will bend the strings
and bring the dials into thrall. His mojo
will slide up and nudge you. Cody'll get inside
and fuck you up, all sharp and flat and blat,
and never stop smiling. He's seven kinds of wrong.
Music has rules just to smack sin into fun, a dance,
a fall. Sprawled on the deck, the sun scorching your eyes,
mouth's bleeding, probably concussed and shouldn't
sleep, and something beating in your mind could kill you,
but move those legs just right, spit a croon, and you'll rip into a grin.

"For now, Elvis can meet and talk with his fans."

Elvis is a mess. That cowlick won't stay down.
Pimples dot his neck. His hair glints
of the gold he was born with. Next year

he'll dye it black; someone decides
it'll photograph better. Here in
1956, he's learning the poses: moodily shirtless

in bed, kissing a girl in a dim hallway,
seated at an upright, fingers brushing
the keys. It's so we can see the secret birth,

the king-to-be. Whence came that beanstalk vision:
the skill of some photographer, the colonel's
gin-eye? Even if '56 is the last time he'll wear

his own light hair, and shop in record stores
alone and slow-dance with his high school girl,
normal's gone with the Tupelo shotgun shack,

gone with Jesse, the dead twin. Normal was
some night Mama told him *that hair's
too long,* and *wash that face,* and *grow up.*

Joni Mitchell Does the Security Interview
for My Christmas Bookstore Job and Asks Me
Have I Ever Stolen

I steal only from bars, from cafes,
only what carries coffee or sugar or light.

A china cup, or stoneware, when my first love
left me in Pennsylvania. A crystal trifle bowl

which, slipping, I dropped in the lot
into a million stars. Barely a month ago,

a candle from a club where I was drunk
on love: different friends, a different Richard.

Did I need that candle, or just want it?
You can keep the job, take the candle

if you need it. I'd steal those coins for the
Wurlitzer, too, if I could reach into the radio;

but now I'm resting my head on my arms
three hours before the interview, wondering

if nine bucks an hour is worth it, if anything
is worth it but music. I can't steal music.

It carries our ages, the lines of nineteen
and that old quilt and mirrors;

older, watching, hearing death come back
and carry them off—even your voice

dark, beautiful darker, cracking, Joni:
impossible to gather such stars to make sugar.

Blessing

After we got our VIP wristbands, they led us through
to meet Jesus. The green room was smaller
than we expected. He had changed from his robes
into a chambray shirt and Dockers, his feet
modestly clad in white socks and Tevas.
He still had that aura, though. The scent of cloves
and mown grass. I got snookered into taking
camera after camera to shoot souvenirs. The old
grip-and-grin. It seemed polite to ask for a photo
of my own. His embrace was warm, brotherly,
only a bit damp, and I felt supreme love and deep
foolishness in equal portions. My companions yelled
Say Christmas! I murmured *I feel stupid.*
The Lord said *Everyone feels stupid. It's OK.*

Carom

*Also known as ajwain, the spice called carom is consumed
as tiny brown oval fruits, which are often mistaken for seeds.*

I thought the seal was good, the contents secure,
just spice for a curry, but then the tiny
flying-up and then the segmented
grains-not-grains and then
shock as I closed the tin,
threw it away,

but not before
my friend sniffed it (as had been
the occasion for my finding it, when
it surfaced on a cooking show, in a scone
or biscuit—and then my riffle through the herbs
and salts as I faintly remembered a long-ago exotic

gift, and then): what if she and I
had inhaled that illicit life and it were to grow? Our love

an infection, rampant with larvae and freed winged victories
and carcasses and the seeds

of something altogether different, aromatic
and strange, something
chronic we'd learn
to live with.

Little Christmas

It's something you hold in your hands,
a crooked pinky for a Wise Man,
palms under the manger. The pocket

savior, big enough to stop a bullet,
baby enough to love. When the fuss
is over, it's the dust that remains:

twigs, rough robes, the soft eyes of sheep.

Smoke

Dear Eleanor, 20 years ago you saw me off home with nine
reams. I copied everything, not sure what mattered. Every note

scribbled by your sister, the Diva: her passport, insurance card,
fan letters. It's not her fault or yours I failed. A good sister

you were, leaving Surrey for Sydney to try to save her. But
the Diva's life was deadly, and then there you were,

left on the edge of a city you didn't choose, among artifacts
yours and not yours, householder serene among surfer-boys

who paid their board with horticulture, two cats, an Airedale
who looked like hers, green glass jars, books with bent edges,

smudgy plates. When I think about running barefoot
through brambles in pursuit of the dead, what was it for? There

you were, burning your delicate expat skin in the back garden
of a morning, beside your sentinel dog, as you teaed and toasted

and smoked and worked the crosswords under the jacaranda—which
I wanted to be a bird, so onomatopoietic was its name

I could hear its cry—and there I was, feigning jet lag,
huddling in a dented iron bed, cast up on the wreck

of your back room, too shy to do the job I'd set myself.
You who added orange juice to the sauce, who sussed out

my love of words, who didn't lord her fame-adjacent past,
who with your surfers offered me the beach—only

once everyone was half awake and half sober and half
dressed and the cars were sorted, there was nowhere left

on Bondi, so we drank. Tonight, I don't remember our interviews
about the Diva. I remember where you kept the ashes

of your childhood dog. I remember you holding the marabou dress
she wore at her last concert, how I wouldn't touch it,

its green-blue plumes drifting. The night we talked, I remember
the game you taught me, how you'd win, shuffle, win again, crack

a wide-eyed smile. The night you laid out the thin paper, broke
and hollowed a cigarette, spread its flakes in a line, sprinkled them

with greener leaf from a baggie. Do they call them baggies
where you live? Or where you came from? So asea was I, so

hopelessly American, so nominally straight, as your firm fingers
pushed the paper tight under the leaves, curled the joint. I said no

when I could have said yes to so much. Now I drink your tea, my
lapsang souchong. I, who never smoked, let it char me, test myself

against its embers as I remember how you, lady of the farthest place
from home I'll ever be, slipped your small tongue from your lips

and lightly, evenly, brushed the edge before that final twist.

Relinquish

Not for a ribbon of earrings, innumerable gold jars. Not for
a lifetime of Richard Thompson concerts, front row, guitar side.
Not for perfect knowledge, dark chocolate, the skeleton key

would I give up the weight of this hand upon my thigh,
here in the sunrise of our senescence, on an ocean
that gets its blue from mystery, its salt from souls.

Not for anyone. Not for the softest sheets. Not for a face
that breaks hearts. Not for immunity relinquish

even the lamest of jokes, the oldest of directionless
secrets, a boast with a belch in the middle, if uttered

in the voice I first heard in my sleep and never forgot.

Two Texas Folk Films

I.

The breeze blows Tracy's hair and her summer dress, painted with lyrics. She dances with it. Her skin shows no bruises. Her voice thins, thickens. Her partner in all things has been knocked off the earth, and she will go on living. Watching the video, after months away from music, I remember what I loved about performance, from the front row. Every molecule so visibly troubled, as God's hand troubles the waters. Pain to paint: every drop of blood a shade of red or brown.

II.

How I was a tumbleweed with a map. How I landed in Texas for a conference, then played hooky after nightfall, took a drive on the flat cheek of unknown Texas to some other part of the state down roads named for creeks and farm machines. How, after dark, the dry dirt glowed as if waiting for Neil Armstrong to plant his rigid ever-flying flag: lit by headlights, lit by occasional peeks of moon, lit then, at my destination, by trees strung with white Christmas by the yard. How I carried a Colorado beer into a shiny drunk crowd. How my purpose, my favorite trio, appeared and turned the sky around and disappeared as the audience disappeared into the shadows of shacks and kiosks. How I spoke to Simon in the sound booth, in the electric boneyard, only a buzz clinging to cottonwoods. How much a handclasp means in such strangeness. How I returned to the rent-a-car in the makeshift parking lot, to the car-lit dust, to the sleepers. How I stayed too long at the fair.

Disco Dance Party at the Adult Guitar Camp

The next day, we looked at each other
    differently, as if traces of gel-clad light
        lingered on our skin. We knew our bodies,

and each other's, could bend more ways
    than our quotidian days demanded.
        Some of us were sore for it. Primarily,

        we were pink. You know, that feeling
    when you run into your pharmacist, or
the music teacher, or someone's visiting brother—

someone who was in your bed, once and only,
    last night—and remember six or seven things
        and smile at how precious we are.

Pam Plays That Tiny Violin

I'm a stubborn noise bumping against the chair legs. I'm a whine.
I'm a bumble. I'm never going to get off this island. I'm walking off
the earth, where the road meets the bridge. I can see the rail. In Russia,

there are forty-two sects that believe in spirits who dress in black
and slither from cupboards at night to sit on your face in your bed.
I don't know if that's true. I heard it somewhere as I did a one-eighty

and walked along the shoulder and into the city where I buy my bread
every other day and still no one knows my name. Once, on the bus,
a man sat on me. I am invisible, and this is why I scream. People think

it's the wind, tighten the belts of their London Fogs. I always leave
my gloves at home. You always hurt the one you love. You can hurt
the ones you don't love, too. Feel free. I am full of what I call poetry. I am

full of hurt and clouds and claws and corridors and I will not, I will not

Notes

The title of the book comes from a chance encounter with the last line of Lawrence Durrell's poem "Echo": "O echo is everywhere, the unbeckonable bird!" Paul Ghosh quoted it in reference to our mutual friend Richard Thompson.

"The Sylvia Plath Tattoo" draws on art seen here: sylviaplathink.tumblr.com/

"It Seemed a Good Idea": The "faces" can be seen here: archive.richardthompson-music.com/catch_of_the_day.asp?id=492

"Dave and the Wolverine": Dave Carter (August 13, 1952–July 19, 2002), with his partner Tracy Grammer, was a maker of what he called "postmodern mythic American folk music." He died of a heart attack in Hadley, Massachusetts, shortly before he and Grammer were to perform at the Green River Festival. His last concert was at Jammin' Java in Vienna, Virginia, on July 17, 2002.

"Oliver Schroer's Last Invention": Oliver Schroer (June 18, 1956–July 3, 2008) was a fiddler, composer, and teacher, with an eccentricity that almost matched his brilliance. The video of "finger shaving" is here: www.youtube.com/watch?v=u3H_gE53RII

"I Am Background": Based on an experience on the second day I worked on *VEEP,* season 4. I don't think it ever made it to air.

"'For now, Elvis can meet and talk with his fans.'": Based on the documentary *Elvis '56* (1987). The title is quoted from the narration of the film.

Acknowledgments

I extend my gratitude to the publications and venues in which these poems have appeared, some of them in slightly different form.

Beltway Poetry Quarterly: "Shake, Alabama"
Delaware Poetry Review: "Mine," "The Problem with Chickpeas,"
    "Watching Game Shows, Early Morning, Living Room"
Fledgling Rag: "Sweet Cider Beloved"
Gargoyle: "Carom," "Oliver Schroer's Last Invention," "Pam Plays That
    Tiny Violin," "Small Repair," "The Essential Man," "Two Texas Folk
    Films," "Whip-Smart"
Northern Virginia Review: "Mallows"
Opossum: "Big Snooker," "Blessing," "'For now, Elvis can meet and talk
    with his fans.'"
Tinderbox Poetry Journal: "Omphaloskepsis"

"Bootleg Dharma" was included in *IOTA Poetry Series 10th Anniversary Reading* (CD/booklet) (rec. 2014; publ. 2015).

"Conjuring Mark Sandman" appeared with an artwork by Denise Paolella in the Ekphrasis project (The Writer's Center, 2016).

"In Which I Am Mad at Flowers Because Paul Is Dying" appeared in *Gathered: Contemporary Quaker Poets* (Sundress, 2013).

Special thanks to the Maryland State Arts Council for a 2017 Individual Artist Award.

About FutureCycle Press

FutureCycle Press is dedicated to publishing lasting English-language poetry books, chapbooks, and anthologies in both print-on-demand and Kindle ebook formats. Founded in 2007 by long-time independent editor/publishers and partners Diane Kistner and Robert S. King, the press incorporated as a nonprofit in 2012. A number of our editors are distinguished poets and writers in their own right, and we have been actively involved in the small press movement going back to the early seventies.

The FutureCycle Poetry Book Prize and honorarium is awarded annually for the best full-length volume of poetry we publish in a calendar year. Introduced in 2013, our Good Works projects are anthologies devoted to issues of universal significance, with all proceeds donated to a related worthy cause. Our Selected Poems series highlights contemporary poets with a substantial body of work to their credit; with this series we strive to resurrect work that has had limited distribution and is now out of print.

We are dedicated to giving all of the authors we publish the care their work deserves, making our catalog of titles the most diverse and distinguished it can be, and paying forward any earnings to fund more great books.

We've learned a few things about independent publishing over the years. We've also evolved a unique, resilient publishing model that allows us to focus mainly on vetting and preserving for posterity poetry collections of exceptional quality without becoming overwhelmed with bookkeeping and mailing, fundraising activities, or taxing editorial and production "bubbles." To find out more about what we are doing, come see us at www.futurecycle.org.

The FutureCycle Poetry Book Prize

All full-length volumes of poetry published by FutureCycle Press in a given calendar year are considered for the annual FutureCycle Poetry Book Prize. This allows us to consider each submission on its own merits, outside of the context of a contest. Too, the judges see the finished book, which will have benefitted from the beautiful book design and strong editorial gloss we are famous for.

The book ranked the best in judging is announced as the prize-winner in the subsequent year. There is no fixed monetary award; instead, the winning poet receives an honorarium of 20% of the total net royalties from all poetry books and chapbooks the press sold online in the year the winning book was published. The winner is also accorded the honor of being on the panel of judges for the next year's competition; all judges receive copies of all contending books to keep for their personal library.

www.ingramcontent.com/pod-product-compliance
Lightning Source LLC
Chambersburg PA
CBHW070011100426
42741CB00012B/3201